DREAMS
DO/oodle
COME
TRUE

VINCE**PALKO**

Dreams DOodle Come True

Contents

Introduction

Nearly 25 years ago, as I sat in a cold classroom in Akron, Ohio, as a sophomore in high school, I stumbled on something that would change the course of my life forever. Keep in mind, this was way before vision boards, way before the movie, *The Secret*. Some may call what I was doing "daydreaming." I call it **Dream Doodling**.

I was fortunate to have parents, coaches, and instructors who cared about my success. These people were instrumental in my success on the athletic field and later in life. They all were amazing teachers of many of life's greatest secrets to success.

> *I was practicing this success principle without knowing what I was doing!*

When I look back, I'm also aware of another key component of my success. I had something else guiding me. Something internal. Something intangible. Something magical. This was my **own intuition**. Later, I discovered how crucial doodling and goals were to my success. Little did I know I was practicing this success principle from an early age without knowing what I was doing! That process became the foundation for this book. I call it a *Dream Doodle*.

A Dream Doodle is a magical flash of intuition that pours out of you and transforms itself into a scribble on a paper that becomes a fortune-telling message for what's to come in your future. Just like an architect uses a blueprint to build lofty skyscrapers, you can build the life of your dreams with these mini-blueprints.

Big dreams and little dreams manifested from these doodles. I attracted new iPods and an ideal mate. I quit my corporate job, wrote a book, played pro football, created the perfect small business, lived in a foreign country, dropped over 40 pounds, ran a marathon, made hundreds of thousands of dollars, and acquired many more items. I've shared this process with countless groups of people through the years — athletes, business folks, fitness seekers, and entrepreneurs, to mention a few.

One day, my 6-year-old, Georgia, asked me to speak to her class and teach art. I agreed, but I wanted to teach them more than just art. I wanted to share how I became a pro athlete through the use of doodling. I wasn't sure how they would handle the information, as it's heady stuff.

Like little sponges were working inside their minds, these kindergartners listened intently and crafted wonderful works of art relating to their dreams. Some scribbled athletes, some doctors, and others teachers. They magically pulled them from inside and scratched them out on their vanilla-colored papers.

Everyone ate up the art lesson! Everyone also devoured the full session of goal setting and life planning that I presented – all through my simple way of connecting with them through the Dream Doodles.

> *When I experienced kindergartners connecting with this message, I decided to write this book.*

Children have grand dreams, and it's our responsibility to help foster them. Sometimes as parents, we have a tendency to limit what we teach our kids, believing they are too young for the message. However, the day I experienced **kindergartners** connecting with this message was the day I decided to write this book. It's time to give back.

My vision? To craft a resource for kids of all ages, young and old, who could benefit from capturing the seemingly "impossible" dream. Now, if you're thinking that you're too old for this kind of planning, think again. Walt Disney sketched the layout for the Disney World theme park on a napkin.

You never know how the world will transform from your own magical doodles.

One day, that person who believes that anything is possible may find the hair on the back of her neck standing straight up, delighting in the fact she achieved her dream and vision. That's why you are holding this book in your hands.

This is the culmination of 25 years of learning, experimenting, and applying the techniques that I am about to reveal. You might say I have a formula, a secret blueprint, for creating success that's as simple as an artist creating a "paint by numbers" portrait of their dreams. You would be correct.

The key is opening your mind to dreams buried deep within and dusting them off so we can begin this wonderful journey together. Grab your box of pencils and let's begin.

Let's turn some doodles into reality!

When you watch a young child draw, you understand that anything can be created and that people are often bigger than houses. Be more childlike.

Chapter 1 ────────────/

Visualization is Dead

Back when rock and roll was "rock and roll," some of the biggest bands declared that rock and roll was dead – The Who, Neil Young, and many more, I'm sure.

But one thing was for sure – **rock and roll was not dead.** It was alive and thriving. Yet maybe this was their way of saying that the new crowd can't jam the same. Not true.

Music changed and morphed ... and then changed and morphed some more – to the point where most kids today can't stand rock and roll of the '70s. American Idol hip-hop stars are the rage.

Where am I going with this? Good question! Visualization is not dead, but a new breed of success experts is galloping into town. And I am pleased to be one of them. Some even call me the "new sheriff" because I make the imagination process a lot easier and fun.

And this all comes from simple sketches and doodles of your future success. When your mind proactively takes charge of directing your thoughts on a daily basis, good things happen to you, your company, your family, and even your kids.

The old success experts served their purpose in time. And by no means do I slight them in any way. Yet, just like rock and roll, there is also a more modern success style of music filling the airwaves — a message that resonates with your entire being.

And the idea of focusing on what you want to bring into your life is never clearer and easier to do than with the power of a picture.

About 80% of our learning and how we experience life comes in through our visual channel. So there is incredible power in the visualization process, using pictures to propel us into the future — a future we desire more than anything.

You may have heard the expression, "A picture is worth a thousand words." I believe that a picture is worth *a thousand dreams coming true.* And one that focuses you on your personal vision is worth a zillion bucks.

And here's why.

In *Psycho Cybernetics*, Maxwell Maltz says:

> Acquiring new information is passive. Experiencing is active. When you "experience," something happens inside your nervous system and your midbrain. New neural patterns are recorded in the gray matter of your brain.

Now, what does this mean? When you read or hear new information, you're merely gathering it, or "acquiring" it, as Maltz says. When you interact with a Dream Doodle, not only do you **experience** the scene in your head unfolding more fully, but you are also instantly focused on the vision. And in essence, you **skip a few steps** to get you in the proper feeling state and on the path to success.

And when you experience it and new pathways open ... bingo, baby – that's when change happens.

Professional athletes use visualization all the time. They picture themselves scoring a touchdown or hitting a home run. Salespeople visualize making a successful presentation and closing the deal. My tools support you in any of these areas and more. Because of the simplicity, many of my clients enjoy Dream Doodles. They are so simple that a child can understand them – at least that what my clients tell me.

Chapter 2 ——————————/

You Can't Draw a Straight Line? So What?

I can't tell you how many times I've heard this: "Wow, you're an artist! I wish I could draw."

The truth is that **everyone is born an artist**. But over time, we just forget how to do it. Or the rust accumulates so much that we don't know where to begin.

When I spoke to my daughter's kindergarten class, I asked how many of them considered themselves artists. And just as I pronounced the letters, A-R-T-I... *every* child's arm flew up.

That experience was the polar opposite of another talk I had with some high school students. When asked the same question, only a third of the students' hands went up.

Why is this?

Somewhere along the way though, we stop thinking of ourselves as artists – for whatever reason. And perhaps at the same time, we lose a bit of childhood wonder and optimism.

Kids are born with 100% creativity. It runs through their veins. But over time, they lose large percentages of this. By the time they are teenagers, they have 50% or less. A number of factors impact this – parents, peers, and other outside influences squelch the creativity out of them.

When you look at a child, these little creatures are just **so happy**. The reason why is simply because these little beings **create**. And create they do, every day.

Kids react to the question, "Who here considers themselves an artist?"

Chapter 3 ⟋

You Don't Have to Be da Vinci to Draw

Everyone is born an artist. And if you've lost it, you can certainly get it back. Now, it's not like I'll be asking you to illustrate like da Vinci in order to see your dreams manifest. The initial sketch I created back in 1987 looks raw and unrefined. I was nowhere near where I am today in terms of my art skills and talents. Yet that picture spoke to me in ways that no other words (or goals) could at the time.

Putting yourself into a relaxed, childlike state is ideal for manifesting your dreams.

My oldest can while away the hours, not noticing where the time goes. That state of mind is exactly what's required when you want more success, money, love, and happiness in your life. The belief that **anything is possible**. The sense that time doesn't matter.

Primo Art Instruction Leveraged for Success

In college, I had one professor who had a very sound approach to teaching – far better than any other professor at that school. He was my sculpture teacher, Sean Morin. He drilled us with the confidence and swagger of most championship coaches. Yet he was an artist, and a damn good one.

I remember working on my first project, chipping away at my sculpture. I was frustrated because what I was creating wasn't turning out exactly as I'd drawn it on my sketchpad.

We were asked to sketch the object that we saw in our mind – the piece we wanted to create from stone. First, we had to draw it from three different angles. This is pretty tough when you've never even seen what you are about to create.

At one point, I got frustrated with my piece. I set the chisel down and went to talk to Sean. He said, "Vince, let's see your pre-sketches." I showed him and he said, "These are great."

But the next thing he said changed my life forever:

"As long as you can put thought to paper in the form of a two-dimensional drawing, you can bring it to life in the form of a three-dimensional object."

With that newfound encouragement, I went on to create exactly what I saw in my mind. It was one of those orgasmic creative moments where I stepped back and said, "Whoa!"

That instruction not only enhanced my sculpting abilities, but it impacted my athletic performance. I applied that phrase to drawing images of athletic success. This was one of the dots that connected what became known as the Dream Doodling process. It was another example of how real life followed my own blueprint, first drawn on canvas.

This became my springboard for success later in life.

Words, affirmations, visualizations, and meditations are all terrific forms of personal development. But don't overlook the power of pictures and how they can change your future.

Chapter 4 ———————/

The Magic of Drawing Your Dreams

The last point of the previous chapter is most important because **we all think in pictures**. But when you **draw in pictures,** you bypass the conscious mind that tends to hold you back, and you speak directly to your subconscious. That's where all the **magic** happens.

> *You won't be da Vinci in a month, but stick figures and shapes will communicate with you like the cave paintings did with our ancient ancestors.*

I look forward to teaching you the art of Dream Doodling. So if you've always wanted to learn how to draw again, now's your chance to finally do it! There's no time like the present to learn something that can draw success into your life.

And if you really can't even draw a straight line... no worries. We'll cover that soon.

You'll be amazed when I reintroduce you to that long-buried talent of yours, just waiting to burst onto the scene. Will you be da Vinci in a month? Probably not. But it doesn't matter! These simple stick figures and shapes will communicate with you like the cave paintings did with our ancient ancestors about folklore, hunting strategies, and so on.

When you combine your newly rediscovered drawing skill with the knowledge that **you have the power to bring anything to life**, you'll no longer express yourself with mere wishes to the world. Now you'll be announcing powerful **commands** to the universe.

Chapter 5 _____/

How to Program Your Mind Without Real Work

If you're wondering if you can use photos as well as illustrations, the answer is yes. Use anything to get your mind thinking about your future vision. I would never limit you and your strategy for attracting things into your life to make it better. For me, whenever I get the chance to draw the ideas percolating in my head, it's a clearer vision for me to rally around. A great second is using photos – or what have become known as "vision boards."

When I was growing up, the walls in my room were plastered with success imagery – everywhere. It was enough to make a feng shui clutter queen go berserk. You see, wallpaper or paint didn't cover the walls – **sports magazine cut-outs of all my athletic heroes did**.

When most self-improvement experts talk about success, they stress the importance of writing a goal. But this isn't how I achieved success. And in my mind, writing goals is only a fraction of the equation, especially since we all internalize information in different ways. No two brains are the same. We have different channels that we pull information from.

I've always considered myself a visually oriented person. And most people are this way. Show someone a PowerPoint that's all words and they may fall asleep. But fill it with photos and funny cartoons, and you'll engage their minds in a dynamic way. If you picked up this book because you just read the cover, chances are you are a visual person.

Chapter 6 ————————/

A Bedroom Built for Greatness

Being a lover of sports, I subscribed to *Sports Illustrated* when I was growing up. The photos were amazing, and I looked forward to each week's copy, especially in football season. But I did more than just read the articles and store away each edition.

I cut out the photos of my favorite athletes: Clay Matthews, Jerry Rice, Chris Spielman, Howie Long, and Lawrence Taylor. I cut out photos of other athletes who inspired me too — Carl Lewis, Jackie Joyner-Kersey, and Mary Lou Retton. And "Ahh-nold."

And I taped these all over the walls. The room looked like a full-color action-shot montage. You couldn't even see the wall paint beneath.

So imagine this: **Every morning, still in a dream-like state, my eyes would open and I'd see all the images of my heroes surrounding me, smiling, laughing, competing.** I'd sit in this dreamy state and think how wonderful it would be to be a champion athlete like my heroes.

When I went to bed at night, I'd lie there and look around. Those pictures were the first and last things I saw when I went to sleep and when I woke up.

My eyes traveled around the room to hundreds of energized action poses, studying each one. I observed the facial expressions, muscle tones, muscle movements, and so on.

Little did I know that I was programming my mind for success.

But these images provided the championship mindset I needed to become a great athlete. How could I not? I was swimming in their essence and energy every time I set foot in that room! That essence rubbed off something fierce to make me a standout linebacker.

(As I found out later, LeBron James did the same. He had a Michael Jordan wall, a Kobe Bryant wall, and another one devoted to a mixture of other basketball players. I made a mental note of this while watching his movie, *More Than a Game*.)

This is another way of communicating through your visual channel to reach success. It's simply **setting a visual target** for your mind to focus on.

Try it for yourself. Cut out images of your "heroes" and hang them where you can see them often. I'm here to tell you – it works.

Chapter 7 _____/

One Shocking Picture that Showed Me How to Create Success On Demand

I always had a dream of playing football. It was my first love, dating back to watching the Cleveland Browns on Sunday afternoons with my father and two brothers.

The trouble was that on the JV football team, I hadn't seen much of the field. This frustrated me beyond belief because I just knew I had skills to contribute. But instead of complaining or whining about it, I used my creative imagination.

Something told me to create a picture of what I wanted to achieve.

But before I share what exactly I created, let me tell you a quick story.

In December 1992, I was home for the holidays. Just the week before, I had helped my college football team win a "nail-biter" in the California Raisin Bowl against Fresno State.

While my mom was preparing the house for the holidays, I slipped upstairs to go digging. What I was searching for I can't exactly remember, but **what I discovered would change my life forever.**

I was just rifling through my closet looking for something I thought was important at the time. But I saw a dusty brown box with a black Sharpie scribble reading "High School." I ripped it open, curious to know what was inside. I pulled out a red folder and found a drawing I had created during my sophomore year at St. Vincent-St. Mary. The penned image of a football player standing in a college uniform glared back at me.

> *I found a drawing I had created during my sophomore year. The penned image of a football player standing in a college uniform glared back at me.*

The athlete wore number 35. He had a crew cut. His sleeves were knotted up, because colleges didn't have form-fitting jerseys back then. The expression on his face was filled with intensity and excitement. There was an autograph just to the right of the drawing. The signature represented one fan's request to go with the drawing, which was really an image of this player caught in time. And the hair on the back of my neck shot straight up.

This drawing was me! And it was me in five years. **I had sketched that image of myself** one cold rainy day in high school of my dream to play Division I college football.

I believe there are no accidents, and this image was the vision of a boy who wanted more than anything to accomplish his dream.

The power of that sketch carried me to a career in football that most could only dream of. As soon as I was done with this drawing, I had taped it to my locker door. Every day when I exchanged my books or grabbed my lunch, **that image spoke to me. Like an architect using a blueprint to build a giant skyscraper, that image directed my subconscious mind down the path to success.**

Even though I never played more than a handful of plays my sophomore year, the very next year I was starting varsity. And this is no slouch of a school! LeBron James and many other talented athletes passed through the halls of St. Vincent-St. Mary. Here, I helped defeat Massillon – a cross-town football factory – for the first time in my school's history. That year we also won State. And this was just the start of an illustrious career in the sport I loved so much.

That cold day in my sophomore English class, the first Dream Doodle was born.

Thirty years later, this image would serve as the teaching point for thousands of boys and girls around the globe.

1987   1994

Chapter 8 ————————————

My Dream to Be
A Champion Athlete
Came True

This is the picture I drew of myself…and how it became a reality.

When I looked at the sketch I had drawn and compared it to the photo of me starting as a redshirt freshman at Bowling Green State University, it hit me like a tidal wave…my youthful dream of playing Division I football on a full scholarship had come true!

> *...whatever I created on paper in the form of an illustration, I could also bring to life.*

And seeing the bowl patches I had illustrated on my shoulders in the old sketch astounded me even more! Just a few weeks before finding that sketch in the attic, I had started in a bowl game as a freshman! At that moment, I began to realize that **whatever I created on paper in the form of an illustration, I could also bring to life. It would manifest into reality virtually overnight.**

After that trip to the attic, I began experimenting with sketches and drawings.

The week before an important football game, I'd use visual imagery to harness my mental focus and preparation. I would draw action-oriented pictures. How I wanted to tackle a running back and knock his head off…I'd draw it. Or how I wanted to blast through the line and sack the quarterback… I'd draw it.

Then when game time came around, the sketches came to life right in front of my eyes. I simply focused on the image. Then I imagined the action. Or heard the crunch. **By having something in front of me to focus on visually, my mind-power took a quantum leap forward.** And soon I was succeeding on a major scale.

I led the team – and the league – in tackles. I was nominated for the Butkus Award. I was selected captain my junior year. And 12 years later I still held many records as a defensive player at BGSU.

But success didn't stop there. Over the years, I used this secret to become a champion athlete, shave fat from my body, and attract money like iron dust to a 500-pound magnet.

So these last couple of stories are examples of attracting a childhood dream during college years. This next set of stories pertains to a different topic set in the same timeframe.

Read on to discover what I'm talking about.

Chapter 9 ———————/

Drawing Your Soul Mate to You

The amount of singles in the world is astounding. Just look at the online dating sites and you'll see that there are plenty of "fish" (or singles) out there in the ocean looking for their ideal mates.

(And yes, this big tough guy is going to write about the topic of love. Vincent is going to unleash his romantic Italian side. This is something you won't see from any other success gurus!)

I recently finished a cartoon for an AdToons client named Tom, and that got me thinking…about love. He's in the "relationship building" business and wanted a cartoon to promote his products.

Anyway, this one image made me think of a sketch I created years ago, and the power it had in attracting my first love. I'm going to share that story – and more. I want to show you that **the power of Dream Doodles isn't limited to just finances, fitness, career, and success. It can**

attract your ideal soul mate as well. Now, if you're already in a fabulous relationship, be grateful for the amazing qualities you enjoy about your partner. Maybe even think about qualities you would want to add to spice things up even further.

Do I claim to be the Dr. Phil of your relationship? Heck, no. I'm no expert in that field. Relationships are something I'm always working at and learning from. But I do believe that **I can show you how to attract that perfect someone**. In every relationship I've had, I consciously written down what I wanted in a partner. And as time passed, I attracted that person to me. Yes, the qualities that were on my radar at the time always surfaced in the mate that I drew to me. And it will happen for you too.

So, on to the fateful first sketch that opened my eyes to the art of attraction using a visual.

Super Powers at Your Fingertips

When I was a freshman in college, a girl I really liked dumped me. Can you relate? I was frustrated and mad. Mad that I had let myself fall for her. As I sat at my tiny desk in my tiny dorm room trying to forget her, I picked up the school paper, the *BG News*. I turned to the sports section. And bang. One photo jumped out at me.

What I saw was an amazing woman blocking a volleyball spike. I immediately took out a pen and sketched the picture I saw. I wasn't sure why. I was intrigued with her, and at the same time fascinated with the power that the picture had flying off it. I've always been mesmerized by photos where greatness is slowed down to a still picture. Wow. I drew that picture all through lunch. I had to eat before going to an off-season workout, but I was so consumed by what I saw and so caught up in my drawing that I lost track of time. I tucked it into one of my class folders and went off to train with my pals.

It's funny how this stuff works. Time passed, and one day, I was eating in a cafeteria by myself when I saw an attractive girl sitting with one of the football walk-ons. I was envious. I watched them. Later, I asked the guy about her and if they were dating. "Nope," he said, "she's just a good friend." And that was it. I never asked how to get in touch with her or anything. Just went on my way.

Now, every winter my football team did "early morning workouts." While the rest of the campus snoozed away in their warm cozy beds, athletes head out at 5 am in frigid temperatures to go to the fieldhouse for conditioning drills. One morning, we finished with suicide sprints – exercises fit more for basketball players than football. As I was running back from my last one, I saw some volleyball players entering the gymnasium wearing their letter jackets. One dark-haired beauty winked at me. What? Yeah, **our eyes met just as I was crossing the finish line and she winked**. I was dead tired, gassed from an intense morning workout. But when then this happened, I was instantly revitalized and energized!

A week passed and I saw her again in the weight facility where all athletes trained. Then I saw her on campus. One night, out with friends, I saw her again. I swallowed my nervousness and walked up to her. We talked the rest of the night. We ended up dating and she became my college sweetheart.

> *Dream Doodles are like goals, but because our minds think in terms of pictures, they work quickly and easily to help you achieve your dreams.*

And then, one of "those moments" happened three months later. I found the folder with the image of the volleyball player I had sketched with my blue ballpoint pen. I looked at it. I sat down hard, reading the caption, with the name of the person in the photo. **The name was the same** of the girl was dating. Holy Toledo!

When I made that drawing, I never knew I would meet her. I was just getting a glimpse into the world of attraction and how it works. Around this time, I was getting other clues about the power of Dream Doodles and their impact on my athletic career.

The visuals work with our subconscious to attract people, places, and things into our existence to support our idea of a better life. They are like goals, but because our minds think in terms of pictures, Dream Doodles work quickly and easily to help you achieve your dreams.

This one was a new discovery because it didn't involve excelling in sports. It's a pretty amazing fact to ponder. There are no coincidences. Everything comes into your life for a reason.

Chapter 10 _____/

Attracting Your Perfect Partner

I'm giving you a tool to use to align the planets in your favor to attract your ideal soul mate. The visual itself is universal and it matters not if you're male or female. The key ingredient in this image is that two people are magnetically attracted to each other, so much so that the guy holds his hands up and the women is still resting effortlessly on his waist. Now you might say, this image is swayed in favor of the man. Why isn't the man holding onto the woman that way? **I believe you cannot get without giving**. So let's assume that the guy has done the work already to warrant such a reaction from the female.

This is how I view the image and how you might too. You can even paste a photo of your face over the picture to represent yourself for extra personalization.

Put it on Paper to Manifest It in Real Life

Modifying your image to make it more personal is important because it involves *you* in the creative process – making you the creator, not the observer. This is now *your* tool.

Next, fill in the area at the right of the cartoon. Or simply write your top 10 list on a piece of paper. This is extremely valuable, because it helps you wrap your mind around the qualities of your future mate. Even if you don't know every detail of what you want, get started. That's key. As you date people and like certain qualities about them, add those qualities to your list. Similarly, you can take away items, ones that once seemed important but aren't any more.

It's an ongoing process until you meet that special someone. When you do meet your soul mate, you'll be amazed at how many items on the list were met or exceeded. If you're married and struggling with your relationship, write down the qualities you're looking for and watch what happens. You may stir curiosity within your partner. They might be upset at what you wrote, but maybe you'll see some improvement in the areas of interest in your Dream Doodle. Give it a try.

Chapter 11 ———————/

Headline: *Major Leaguer Pulls Himself Out of a Slump Fast with Doodles and Designs*

Now ,like a roving *Sports Illustrated* writer, I'm going to let you in on a story. It's a behind-the-scenes look at how a pro player went from a slump to setting a team record in a very short time. The headline could be the same as the title of this chapter.

Lately, most stories of high-profile athletes are negative. This one goes against the grain to show you the positive side of the player.

There are moments in our lives when we meet special people. We know it instantly. When we meet there is a heavenly electric "zap." Part of that electric bond is sharing common interests and experiences.

What I know about high-achieving individuals is they get creative on how to improve their lives. I happened to be in Tampa some time ago with a friend who coaches a few pro players.

On Friday night, I joined my buddy, Matt Furey, for a Tampa Bay Rays game, enjoying a spectacular view in the action seats behind home plate. Matt had recently done some work on mindset coaching with one of the Rays' players, and he'd had a rough night. He went 0 for 4, striking out twice and flying out twice. The next morning, Matt asked if I'd like to tag along to his coaching session with the big-league home run hitter. He didn't have to twist my arm.

We drove to this man's condo on the beach and I wondered how this whole situation would play out. As I said, I believe there are no accidents and that everything happens for a reason. In this case, the answer to my wondering convinced me that I was fortunate to be on this trip.

Carlos greeted us and we shook hands. Matt's son had brought some baseball cards and balls to sign. We walked out to the private pool behind the high-rise condo, where he and Matt would later have their training session. While signing one card, he stopped to look at the back and read the information written about himself. "I never get to read what's on these cards when I'm signing them at the ball park," he said. Hmm, I thought – interesting humble comment.

The four of us chatted while he signed about five baseballs and other material. Then, Matt's son and I headed to the beach. After about two hours, I looked back to the pool area to see Matt standing next to his client, who was holding an imaginary bat, practicing his swings. Shadow hitting – just like shadow boxing – was the drill Matt had given him. He did this while other condo dwellers lounged around the pool watching him. People staring did not faze Carlos one bit.

> *I looked back to see Matt standing next to his client, who was holding an imaginary bat, practicing his swings.*

Key point: Successful athletes are always looking for the slight edge to improve their ability.

High-level athletes also have an uncanny way of keeping their mind open to learning and trying new things. They act like sponges, soaking in all the pertinent information. This particular person had the ability to put himself completely into the exercise, using a thick layer of immunity to the onlookers and their thoughts. He did the drill with enthusiasm and vigor.

Keeping an open mind is the fastest way to improve your life. So many times when I work with young athletes, I ask them who their favorite sports figure is. I'm surprised when I hear, "I'm my own favorite athlete. I don't look up to anyone, really."

To me, this is a sign of being closed off, unwilling to emulate and learn from great athletes who have far superior skills. This is my first clue that someone isn't open to learning how to improve a technique or skill.

Key point: Be open to learning if it's coming from a valid resource.

Anyway, let's get back to observing the session from afar. This high-profile athlete was all about keeping an open mind and learning! Shortly after the shadow-hitting drill, my phone rang. "Vince, come up to the pool when you're done down there," Matt said.

Carlos had never read *Psycho-Cybernetics*, and Matt had just given him a copy of the book. Carlos opened it to a spot that kicked off a conversation about how to get out of a slump by recalling past successes versus past failures. After skimming the page, he exclaimed, "This is what I've been doing! I've been walking to the plate thinking of my past strikeouts and almost dreading being there!"

Matt then asked a few key questions about times when he was successful at the plate. This follows what Matt teaches based on the principles taught in *Psycho-Cybernetics*.

When I joined the conversation, Matt told me how Carlos had creatively used his imagination throughout his career and said, "You're going to enjoy this, Vince." Matt knows how excited I get about creatively generating unique ways to develop goals and the achievement process!

What happened next was an amazing conversation, with three people all talking about success. Not once did Carlos come off as a highfalutin jerk, like some spotlight performers I've met.

Here's the story he shared:

Back in 2007, Carlos was canned from baseball. But he wasn't worried. He had a relaxed confidence. Up until that point, he had always written down his goals in a journal. For example, he'd write, "I'm so grateful and thankful for the _____ that I now have in my life." The blank represented what he was in hot pursuit of.

Key point: Create a power statement that you affirm or write in your journal. Repeat often.

When writing his goals on paper became mundane and rigid, Carlos tried something new. He drew pictures. He'd doodle pictures of himself with a hot bat (a term ballplayers use to refer to being on a hitting streak) and actually wrote **"hot"** on the bat itself. He drew a picture of himself with the number he wanted to wear when he'd play for the Tampa Bay Rays. (Any of this sound familiar?)

Apparently, Dream Doodling works anywhere, any time and for anybody. But the story continues...

Chapter 12 _____/

Using the Creativity and Energy of an "Old School" Graphic Designer To Lay Out Dreams

At one point, Carlos took his creativity to the extreme. Before Tampa ever signed him that year, everyone told him that the Rays were too cheap to pay him what he felt he deserved, considering other players' salaries.

This didn't bother Carlos. He believed so deeply that he took things to the next level. He basically wrote an article. This reminded me of how design layouts were created before layout software (like Adobe's InDesign) was invented.

He cut out the masthead of *USA Today* and pasted it onto a sheet of paper. He cut out photos of himself from previous articles. He created blocks of copy to fit around the photos. He wrote how the story would unfold – what reporter would write and how he would respond. Basically, he composed, designed, and published the entire story way before it ever happened. Then he took the raggedy-edged, pasted-up paper with the clippings to Kinko's and photo-copied it so it would lay flat.

Key point: Find creative ways to spur your imagination to a future event before it ever happens, like a "mind map" to get you to your destination.

When the article was written in real life – **which actually did happen** – Carlos placed the "published" article in his treasure chest with the one he had created. Amazing. (Did you catch the next hint? *He put it in a special place.*)

Key point: Make a designated spot where you'll stow accomplished goals. This way, you have an unlimited source of fuel to put into the tank for future goals.

As it turns out, he got the number he wanted to wear. He got the team he wanted to play for. And (this is a *big* "and"), he got the money he had written in the article – $24 million over three years.

This is a pretty astounding number to pull out of the air for an unemployed ball player. This is also a good example of setting what you believe you are worth and letting the Universe/God serve it. (Speaking of God and your higher power, this man is a deeply spiritual person, and he chose 23 because it represents an important Bible passage for him.)

Key point: Make the Divine, however you perceive it, a part of your goal-setting and achievement process.

This "magic article" was one of many tools Carlos used in order to creatively become his own story. As we left him, he said he was going to stretch, get into the ocean for a while, then drive to the stadium for that night's game.

Key point: Set aside time before your major league event, business meeting, talk, etc., to be by yourself and stretch.

Although we couldn't get to the ballpark that night, we were glued to the TV. What an amazing day, I thought, to have that conversation and then to watch this guy get a huge hit after receiving a workout routine for the mind.

Later that week, I got a message from Matt: "Six homers in the last six games." It took this pro player a mere week to pull out of a slump and break a team home-run record. Plus, he made an attempt to break the MLB record for most home runs hit consecutively. Pretty darn cool.

So how long does it take for a major leaguer to pull out of a slump? In this case, one week! I've always been a believer in this stuff. After experiencing this story, **are you a major league believer now?!**

It's up to you to use your creativity to blast through stuck patterns to reach the dreams you've always wanted to achieve.

Here are four things I picked up from this pro player that you can adapt for yourself:

1) Dream within reason and without reason.
When no one else believed Tampa would give Carlos a big contract, he got one. He believed so much that he literally put together how a feature story might unfold for himself. You have to find the balance between what is achievable in your mind and what's unrealistic.

2) Get creative about the messages that are being delivered to your brain.
If you write, draw. If you draw, write your goals. And if you are really feeling up to it, do both! Do things that activate different parts of your brain.

3) Use variety when a method stops being fun.
Try a new medium such as painting, clay, cardboard cutouts, and so on. If you're stuck, find some kids. They can show you how to be creative.

4) Develop a manifest treasure chest.
A shoebox, a folder, a plastic bag – designate something as your special place to stow your goals and dreams.

Chapter 13 —————————

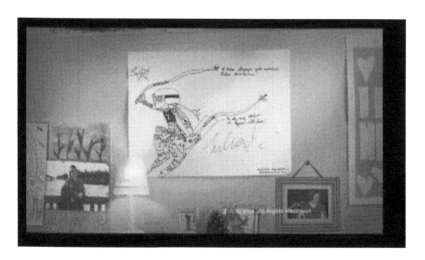

Olympic Skier Sees Shiny Medals At an Early Age

When she was a little girl, skier Julia Mancuso drew a poster of herself as an Olympic medalist.

In 2010, she competed in several events and won a silver medal in a string of tight finishes. Look on YouTube for a Visa commercial about this very thing (search for "Julia Mancuso Visa commercial"). If you're saying, "Well, it wasn't a *gold medal*," this is the talk of someone who has never competed at a high level.

The level of competition at the Olympics is fierce, and Julia performed incredibly. Her young-girl dream came true, and her future is just beginning. Capturing your dreams on paper in the form of a sketch is powerful stuff.

Inspect the drawing. Notice how she drew a picture of herself crossing the finish line, hand raised in the air. She wrote down the actual dream. She signed it as if it were a legitimate contract with herself.

What an amazing story of epic proportions.

Next let's move to a sport a bit *closer to home*. Perhaps you play it. Flip to the other side to find out what it is.

Chapter 14 _____

How to Shave 16-Plus Strokes Off Your Golf Game Virtually Overnight, with No Practice and a Hand-Me-Down Set of Clubs from the 1960s

Not long ago, I went golfing with my brothers and dad. One interesting thing about golf is that you can really pick up on the **negative chatter** that average people create for themselves – especially on the putting green.

Some common phrases heard during putting:
• "Hit it, Alice!" (When a ball comes up short.)
• "I lipped it!" (When the golfer jerks at the last second and misses the cup.)

If these statements are any indication of what's going on inside people's minds, most golfers are in quite a bit of trouble. Not good! As a result, in this round, I wanted to watch my words no matter how ugly or pretty it became. I also planned to apply the drills I used in football to tremendous success – and reap the same results on the course. Thankfully, this technique worked wonders.

After parring several holes, I came up to my best hole. It was 400 yards to the pin. I took out my driver and hit my first shot. The shot went straight down the middle to about 280. On the second shot, I used my wedge to put the ball less than two feet from the cup (see picture for proof).

It was a great shot! After I had a few more holes of draining 20-foot putts and scoring several pars, my dad, who golfs every week and feels that he has hit a ceiling with his game, asked, "Have you been golfing?"

"Only in my head," I said.

"What do you mean?" he asked.

"I see the shot I want to make before I swing. Then it does what I want. If for some reason I make a bad shot, I never say anything bad to myself. I take a deep breath and I say, 'Get back *this* shot, Palks.'"

Most people who golf beat themselves up for *duffing* a shot, and therefore, their game spirals out of control. As for me, I like to do the opposite. **"This game is easy," is actually what I said all day long.** As a result, I trimmed 16 strokes off my game.

> *This time I tried something different. I focused on the ball resting in the exact place I wanted it to go.*

You might think that to be better at something, you need to work twice as hard. **The reality is that you only need your imagination to work for you.** That means a whopping few minutes of thought time a day. No physical effort whatsoever. The week before this story, I played great shots in my head. Also in my head, I heard positive comments from my foursome buddies. I smelled the fresh-cut grass. I recalled great shots made in the past – all of these things **one week before playing the actual match.**

I gained this new insight during that round: In the past, I tried to visualize the path of the ball coming off my club going to the spot I wanted it to go. To my chagrin, no success! There were shanks and slices all over the place. This time, however, I tried something different. I focused on the end target (see photo on previous page) and in my mind's eye saw the ball landing, bouncing a few times, and resting in the exact place

I put it, give or take a few yards. To my amazement, this technique worked extremely well! I shot a 90.

The lesson in this situation is to **focus on the end target, not the projection of your path or how you'll get there**. The desired result will all magically happen, just like your mind creating the perfect swing when you visualize the end target!

What you need to *see* every time you step up to the tee box.

Chapter 15 _____

The Magic Ingredient for Improving Your Golf Game

If golfers did this type of visualization instead of going out to hit a bucket of balls, their game would improve three-fold. No, I'm not talking about investing in a new set of clubs. I'm not talking about subscribing to a set of instructional videos. **I'm talking about practicing breathing**.

"Tell me something new, Vince," I can already hear you say. But listen to me clearly and emphatically: Practice your breathing when you are on the course.

Five Important "Remember to Breathe" Scenarios

1) Before you hit the first shot. This shot sets the tone for the whole match. While others are warming up their swing and stretching, prepare by taking several deep breaths. This will relax you – and ensure a strong, straight first drive.

2) After you hit a lousy shot from the tee box. When you want to toss your club into the lake, breathe and repeat, "I can recover just like Tiger does."

3) Following a wonderful shot anywhere on the course. This step prevents what some golfers call Ego-Inflatus-Maximus. With very full breath you take, you make sure that the hot air doesn't stay in your head, making it swell with cockiness and arrogance.

4) As you approach your well-placed ball in the fairway. Take three deep quiet breaths as your cart pulls up next to your ball. This will ensure consistency. Practice the same for a horribly placed ball and repeat the phrase in #2.

5) As you approach your ball resting on the green. By the time you approach your ball and grip the putter, you should already have taken a few deep breaths.

Repeat, "My mind provides me the perfect swing to allow me to drain this putt. Thank you."

When you combine the breathing tips with picturing the ball dropping right where you wanted it – while you address the ball each time – you'll be amazed at how much your game improves.

Here are the keys to improve your golf game:

1) Focus on the end target. See your ball hitting the turf and bouncing up and down exactly where you want to place it.

2) Tell yourself the game is easy. Picture in your mind preparing and delivering the perfect swing to put the ball exactly where you want it to be in #1. Do not tell others. Keep it to yourself.

3) Breathe. Don't underestimate the importance of breathing on the golf course. Breathing is a perfect mind-leveling tool. If you get a big head from a good shot, proper breathing brings you back to your center point. If you duff a shot and want to beat yourself up, it also eradicates negative thoughts and returns you, again, to your center point.

Chapter 16 ⟍

A Mother-Son Team's Dream Realized

Last year, I wrote an article about a young wrestler who had hopes of winning at the state level. His mother and I crafted a Dream Doodle for them both to focus on. Here's the story:

There was a big sports upset last week. However, this particular upset has nothing to do with an over-hyped college or NFL game. Instead, it takes place on the dusty wrestling mats of Findlay High School and a young junior named Max.

Max wrestles in the heavyweight category, yet he is at a distinct disadvantage, as he weighs only 240 pounds. His opponents weigh at least 285. He has a height advantage, though, with a towering 6'5" frame.

You'd think that all he has to do is to keep his caloric intake above his burn rate so he could gain some weight. But this process is easier said than done. A miniscule three-pound gain is worthy of a celebration, as nothing seems to "stick."

> *Max can take pictures in his mind— an integral component to success.*

Every morning, his mom prepares a hearty breakfast, and Max heads to the gym to work out. Sadly, since he lost his father before he had a chance to get to know him, his mom acts as both mom and dad to her son. Consequently, she knows more about the sport than most other mothers. Also, she diligently ensures that her heavyweight is well fed so he can keep up with his oversized opponents. In many ways, she's like a second coach, as she invested in a personal strength trainer to help "beef him up."

Max is also unique as he has a great painting and drawing ability. As a result, **he can take pictures in his mind – and materialize the images on paper**. This ability is an integral component to success, along with the goals he sets for himself. When Max was ranked #10 in Division II, he had to face an opponent who was ranked number #1. This was a hard-fought battle that lasted 10 minutes ... but when the dust on the mat settled, Max's arm was raised. Holy smoke – he won!

A couple of weeks before that match, his Mom hired me to create a Dream Doodle of Max winning the state championship. In the framed illustration, I tried to capture the pride he would feel when he won this match – and the pride his mom would experience when the two hugged afterward.

Creating a highly emotionally charged picture of the future that does not yet exist is the fastest way to achieve the unachievable.

If Max could continually hold this clearly defined visual, as well as do all the other requirements to succeed, he had every chance to be a state champion – as a junior.

Here are more of his results:

Max *did* make it all the way to state – as a junior and with a 40-to-50-pound handicap in his weight class.

At the state championships, he won every match except for his final one. He wrestled the top athlete from the previous year, but Max didn't win. Now, do you think that this last match was a negative event? Do you think he wallowed in failure mentality? Hell, no! This turn of events could be the best thing to happen to the young man. Why? Because **he'll be back, stronger and more aggressive than before** to grab the state title next year. This "loss" event will most definitely propel him into his college career.

In fact, Max went on to wrestle in Nationals and took fourth place. Eight men are always invited to be national champions – and Max became a part of that group. Scouts swarmed left and right to offer him scholarships to their schools.

How cool is that?

Max's Success Dream Doodle of Winning State

We created this Dream Doodle for his mom. She, of course, had her own goal of seeing her son succeed. I believe that **if you have more than one mind focused on a goal, the end result is an even stronger intention to succeed.** That's the reason why these Dream Doodles are so powerful as they rally entire offices, families, and organizations around a common vision. I believe that when you have many minds aligned to a common goal, you can achieve your desires faster and easier.

Chapter 17 —————————/

Preparing Your Mind to Meet Any Obstacle

In 2003, I decided to run a marathon. Why? Well, when you hang up the football cleats, you don't have many opportunities to sharpen your mental toughness. For example, I used to *purposely* crash into guys who were bigger than me about 85 times per game. So the thought of running 26.2 miles appealed to my desire for challenging both my mental and physical toughness. But it would be no easy feat at 240 pounds.

I chose to run in the Chicago marathon, and I'm glad I did. That city does a tremendous job with its support crew. In fact, the city itself gets behind you. Imagine 1.5 million people cheering you on along the way! It's the biggest sports arena I ever played in. My goal was to score a sub-4-hour run. But I tanked and ran a 4:27. Since my goal was not complete, I set out to run another one the next year.

So I decided to run in the Marine Corps Marathon in Washington D.C. And I drew this doodle a few months before the race. In Chicago, I'd learned how challenging the last leg of the race was going to be – straight uphill for a mile. I first prepared this sketch, and then prepared my mind to meet the challenge head on about a hundred times way before I ever ran it.

This is the image I drew and focused on for three months before the race, preparing my mind for that last hill on the course.

Again, my goal was to run in under four hours. At work, I'd look at this picture and see myself being tired, but having enough energy left to reach my time. I tried to picture the sights and sounds and smells. And this doodle was my doorway into that visualization whenever I looked at it.

Let's cut to the 25th mile, as I approached the dreaded hill. Here's a slice of my experience from my journal:

> **Mile 25** (goal 10:00, actual 10:42) When I looked at my watch, it didn't register right away. I read it again. I was at 3 hours 50 minutes!

I thought, "I've got 1.2 miles to go in under 10 minutes – uphill, in 74-degree weather! And the last mile took me 10:42! Holy crap, I'd better get running!" Fans lined the narrow street and yelled cheers as I passed, but I blocked it all out. The hill I was climbing passed the Iwo Jima monument and then took a left – straight up an even steeper slope. I put my head down and charged! I told myself I wouldn't stop until I got to the finish line, just like I'd programmed my mind using the visual I drew three months before – "Attack!"

For the last mile, I was a machine. Programmed from the work I'd done with my Dream Doodle, I practically sprinted up the last leg of the hill and across the field. I made my time of 3:59:46! What a wonderful feeling.

There's a funny thing about your mind. Even if you have a future event perfectly drawn and planned – just seeing parts of it – you'll still succeed at a higher level than if you'd never doodled to begin with. Doodle your next "long distance-race" and watch yourself shave time from your personal best.

Chapter 18 ———————— /

Losing Weight with a Dream Doodle

At the end of every January, people who set New Year's resolutions are kicking them to the curb. This is especially true for people who say they're going to lose weight. I once hosted a webinar that focused on reaching weight loss goals, and I chose one coaching member to visualize a weight loss Dream Doodle for.

This was the message from the person I selected, Ann:

> Vince, I want to lose 30 pounds, regain my flat stomach, have toned arms and legs, and feel comfortable in a new set of clothes. During my childhood, teenage years, and throughout my 20s and early 30s, I never had a weight problem, but I always thought that if I lost 5 to 10 pounds, that would make me happier. When I look at pictures of myself then, I can't believe I wasted time with those thoughts. I looked fine! I still want those pounds off,

but I also want to be comfortable and not think, "If only I were 5 pounds thinner…" and just be comfortable in my own skin and with my own self-image.

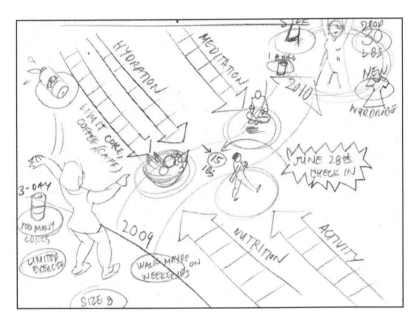

This Dream Doodle is what I drew for Ann. As you can see, we covered many elements of a fitness plan for her to focus on. This may look a bit overwhelming, but if she focused on one item to track then added another and another, the process would help her cut out the bad, supplement new, and add healthy practices to support her intention of getting fit. Basically, create a visual that depicts your current reality and your desired future with a road leading from one to the other. Pick a few (maybe three) key elements to your success and put in a daily/weekly metric for each. Check off the metrics as you complete them as a way to keep score. How am I doing? You can print a new weekly worksheet when you finish the previous week. You could have different intervals, depending on the goal. It might be monthly, quarterly, etc.

Personal Weight Loss Dream Doodle

If you'd like to use this tool for yourself, here are 9 points to help you:

1) Make 8 copies of the Personalized Weight Loss Dream Doodle tool.

2) Mark the top of the pages Week 1, Week 2... all the way to Week 8.

3) Choose one area to track (or several).

4) In each chosen area, write your goal for the week. For example, "I will eat one salad a day." So for the Nutrition arrow, create 7 blocks, one for each day.

5) Track your progress on each arrow by placing an X in the square for the day as soon as you achieve that goal. If you ate a salad that day, mark an X in the box. And continue.

6) Do the same for other items – hydration, activity, meditation, etc.

7) At the end of the week, see how you did. Make an honest assessment of what you did right, where you can improve, and how you can adjust the tool to fit your progress.

(continued)

---

8) See where you are at the end of the week, and create your action plan for the next week.

9) At the end of the 8 weeks, tally up how many days you hit your goal, and divide it by the number of total days. Score your success, and congratulate yourself for taking this challenge!

Chapter 19

The Law of a Crystal-Clear Vision

The other day I logged onto YouTube.com and tuned into a Brian Tracy video.

In the clip, Brian said,

> "All you need to do to raise your self-confidence, your self-esteem, and your level of attainment high is to have an absolute crystal-clear goal and work on it every single day."

One way to create a crystal-clear goal or dream is to draw it on paper, as an architect does before the construction process begins on a house or a building.

Paint a picture in your mind first, then put it on paper. This is the perfect way to keep you motivated and to communicate with your subconscious to activate the Law of Attraction.

What is the Law of Attraction, you ask? It's the magnetic energy of the Universe that draws together similar energies. Another way to say it is "You get what you think about."

Some people have used goals and vision boards to focus their minds to attract what they want in life. These work well if you feel comfortable drawing your own Dream Doodle. But if you can doodle your dreams, look out!

Remember that I told you about my college sculpture professor who said that anything can be created in the form of a three-dimensional object as long as you can draw what's in your mind on paper? I believe that's true not only for creating something from nothing as sculptors do, but for activating the Law of Attraction as well.

A Dream Doodle Takes Shape

Some time ago, after seeing my Dream Doodle in my *Success* newsletter, a coaching client contacted me to create his own Dream Doodle.

Steve said, "The image you drew of what you wanted back then – **you're doing it now!**"

"Yes, isn't that something?" I said, grinning.

If you don't feel comfortable or creative enough to do your own, you can always hire someone to do it for you.

So we worked together to create his vision of a better life. Now you might think "better" means more money. Steve has a job that pays well. But he wants freedom. He's a stock trader on Wall Street and has little time for his five girls. (Five! I thought I was outnumbered with three!)

Anyway, he wanted to continue to serve his company, as he had done successfully in the past. At the same time, he wanted to begin building a better life for himself and his family.

Here is the Dream Doodle I created for him.

Steve's Current Reality:
As a stock trader for a major financial firm on Wall Street, Steve trades companies in emerging markets in South America. He knew that his job had "run its course," and he had started at the bottom and built it up from basically nothing. The challenge had dissipated. I drew this section smaller because I want his focus to be on the rest of the Dream Doodle, not the current reality.

Steve's New Business:

A few years ago, Steve dreamed up his next business
venture. He wanted to do something where he could
incorporate his core competence of buying and selling,
transitioning these skills into a livelihood of his own. He
stumbled upon an idea: Buy and sell domain names.
Supporting his family at the same income was essential. He
planned to move his family out of New York, and when this
happened, he'd be able to get by with less, as New York's cost
of living is through the roof.

Moving the Family:
Steve didn't really know where they might move –
"somewhere out West," I remember him saying. When I
asked him to get specific, he thought maybe Oregon. Even if
he doesn't end up there, it still gives his mind something to
focus on. He can always adjust to wherever they may end up.

The key is to have a plan. You can always modify as you go.

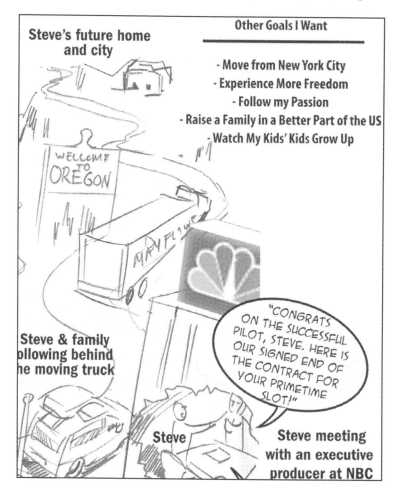

The TV Show:

Steve has a fascinating idea for a TV show and has gone to great lengths to get his script in front of the right people. Keep your eyes peeled for a show called *The Individualist*. Steve has a long way to go, but his foot is in the door, so that's half the battle.

So my challenge was to include everything into one cohesive picture. The Dream Doodle had to include his current reality with his near-term goal of launching "Wall Street Grunts," the business of trading websites. The image also had to include his other goal of his TV show, *The Individualist*, making it to prime time. And finally, I wanted to capture Steve's interest in moving his family out of New York City. I wanted his current reality to be just a slice of the overall real estate of the Dream Doodle. I wanted his main business front and center. This was the top priority to make happen first. Then, the TV show and moving seemed to fall into place.

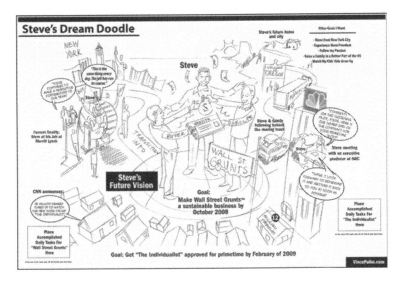

The completed picture of Steve's Dream Doodle

There is a lot of detail in this image. It's almost a Where's Waldo? approach to his vision. **But the important thing is, that Steve has everything mapped out and crystallized**. Now he can spend time with this every day. Even if he doesn't focus directly, the image has planted mental anchors of his future in his mind.

A few years have passed since we co-created this image for Steve. Here is what he had to say about the process:

> I've always been a firm believer in writing down and reviewing my goals on a daily basis, so when I found Vince's product on vision boards, I knew I had stumbled onto something revolutionary.
>
> I soon contacted Vince and, over a two-week period, he reviewed all my goals and forced me to clarify the vision that I wanted for my life. Within a week, he had created a fantastic visual board for my life. The visual board had all of my goals represented, drawn as action sequences. For example, one of my main objectives was to leave my job and to move to another city and, on my vision board, Vince drew a magnificent drawing expressing this.
>
> I placed my vision board in my home where I always would have to look at it. This process of always looking at my vision board made me internalize my goals more deeply than I thought possible. I also have come to believe that **the physical drawings and doodles of my goals enabled me to focus my mind** more profoundly on the goal-setting process and **helped me achieve my goals more quickly than I thought I could.**

How Do You Find Your Passion?

At a seminar, I heard a speaker mentioned that it's good to know what your purpose is here on Earth. Later, I chatted with a guy named Mike before I left for the airport.

The intensity in Mike's eyes was palpable. He knew he was done working for The Man. Yet, at the same time, he didn't know exactly what he was called here to do. He asked me a question I believe many people are thinking: "I know I want to bring my passion to life. I'm just having difficulty figuring out what my purpose on Earth is. How do you find this?"

I said, "Well, I think you have to learn to quiet your thoughts. **You have to be able to put the stresses of the day aside for 'you time.' And then listen to what rises to the surface of your mind**. And as ideas start to percolate, it then becomes 'try time.'

When you experiment with different ideas, eventually something will click for you."

I continued, "I don't believe you become enlightened one day with this strong calling that knocks you off your feet and says, 'Michael! Go now and serve!' I believe it comes with trial and error. You get clues along the way, but it's a process that takes time – time to dial into the exact passion that can become your profession."

"I always knew I wanted to find a way to help people," I told Mike, "but I wasn't sure exactly how. The moment earlier in the weekend when I was on

(continued)

stage speaking to the group, something clicked. I knew this was part of my calling – challenging, inspiring, and motivating folks to become more of what they believed they could be."

Tears welled up in my eyes. And in Mike's as well.

He could feel my energy and emotion coming through. He felt that same energy and emotion. That same desire to make difference was planted in him as well.

So where is *your* passion? Where do *your* interests lie? How do *you* want to impact people? Steve Jobs said, **"Make a dent in the universe." It doesn't have to be a big dent. It can be a tiny one**. But the most important key is that *you* will feel pleased as a pickle working to create the dent.

If you would like a personlized Dream Doodle that works three times better than a vision board, email vince@vincepalko.com and write "I want a Dream Doodle" in the subject line.

Chapter 20 ⟋

Quit Your "Day Job" and the Money Will Follow

Not long ago, I did what most people tell you not to do.

I quit my "day job."

I did this to bring to life what I am meant to do, which is to change the world with my fitness and success products. These fully support my goal of helping people become better physically, mentally, emotionally, spiritually, and financially.

Also, I have a passion for giving my clients "marketing zing" with a unique cartoon flair using my AdToons characters. (See AdToons.com.)

After I quit my job, I thought, "Ah, the first day of the rest of my life – completely on my own!" I also thought, "I have three little ones to support. What project will I tackle next?"

The next thing that came to mind was Tom. He is the man Dan Kennedy talks about in his series *Magnetic Marketing*. Tom became tremendously successful in selling by **adopting the mentality of never going home to eat dinner unless he had made at least one sale**. These were the thoughts racing through my mind.

I drove to a local strip mall to introduce AdToons to some area businesses. Up to that moment, AdToons had served clients all over the country and the world, but not locally. So I thought I'd give the whole belly-to-belly experience a whirl. It's kind of the opposite approach from what most people take. Most start locally and then expand. I grabbed a book from the trunk of my car and walked into a small fitness facility. I met the owner and gave him a copy of my book. He said he didn't need any cartoon services but would keep the book for future reference. So I got back to my car feeling puzzled about what to do next.

When I got home, I found a FedEx envelope on my doorstep, with a return address of the "Millionaire Maker," Dan Kennedy.

My heart raced. I was like a little kid! "*What's inside? What's inside?*" I thought.

I ripped it open to discover a three-page personal letter from Dan inviting me to illustrate his next book, along with a nice check and an opportunity to make a whole lot more dough.

Then I felt it. An overwhelming sense of peace and calm lifted me off the ground, and I heard the words in my head, "Palko, *this* is the beginning of the rest of your life."

It's crazy. I had just been thinking about what Dan had said in his *Magnetic Marketing* course about Tom. The next thing I knew – whamo! a FedEx envelope from Dan appears, inviting me to work side-by-side with him. This story illustrates that when one door closes, another opens.

But the small door that closed paled in comparison to the one that had opened.

For some strange reason, I feel that the opportunity would not have presented itself if I hadn't just taken some action. Often you'll hear that it takes action to reach your dreams, or as Tony Robbins says, "massive" action. Others say that you should take baby steps. I don't agree with either, really. I believe it takes "uncomfortable" action, an action that requires you to leave your comfort zone regularly. **If you push your boundaries of comfort over and over, the universe will open up to your requests.**

So many people feel trapped in their jobs, just as I had for the past six years. Six years is nothing, though. Many people feel this way for 15, 20, or even 30 years. Yuck!

Toward the end of my corporate gig, I'd go to the restroom each day for the sole purpose of reviewing the goals I had set. Then, still in the bathroom, I'd do some push-ups and squats. After that, I had enough energy to get back to work for a few more hours. I did this three or four times a day! And I'd think, "Wouldn't it be cool to work with a big name like Dan Kennedy?"

Now, in case you're thinking that I'm suggesting you quit your day job tomorrow, think again. You need a dream and a plan. And you need to combine exercise with your imagination so you can bring your dreams to life. The exercise component will help your mind enter a trance-like, euphoric state. The mental resistance goes down, which enables you to ramp up your daydreaming possibilities and make them stick in your brain.

But let's go back to that letter from Dan Kennedy. Do you think receiving a message from Dan on the very same day I left my job was a coincidence? Hardly.

As I said, whatever you keep your mind focused on attracts to you the very people, places, things, and events that will support your vision. Re-read the last few paragraphs, and you'll know it was no "co-winky-dink."

My Dream Doodle Visual

I drew this image in 2004. It served as the launch pad for my future success. Thanks to this visual roadmap, I completed my first triathlon – even though I couldn't swim 20 yards before training for it. I wrote several books and "how-to" courses that enabled me to make a handsome living. Ultimately, I broke the chains that were holding me back and left the corporate rat race.

Even if you have no desire to leave your job and work for yourself, you can still use this information to your benefit. Like a child who knows that anything is possible, play with your thoughts and imagination. Steer them where you want them to go, and sit back and watch what happens.

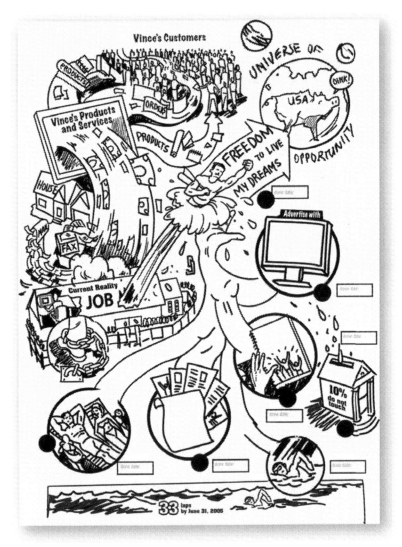

A Dream Doodle created a few years before I quit my day job

Chapter 21 ——————————/

Acres of Diamonds

From time to time, I hear people say that the only way to get ahead is to work two jobs or to work harder. But to make more money and achieve greater wealth, **what it really takes are ideas** – ideas that make you more money, ideas for a business, ideas for a product to sell on the Internet. We live in a global marketplace where anyone and their brother can think of an idea that meets the need of an audience.

How to use this visual: First, make a couple of copies. Put a few in a folder for future use. Take one copy and spend some time thinking about ideas for bringing more prosperity into your life.

This is an amazing feeling – to know that **we all have different life experiences**. We've each lived a life with myriad experiences, and we've all learned different things along the way. So the challenge is to figure out what you know that comes second nature to you. Sometimes the best ideas are right beneath our own schnozzes.

So take time, get quiet, and figure it out. Write one idea on each diamond that appears on your sketch – "Acres of Diamonds." What do you know that others would want to learn? **These are the diamonds that can create additional revenue streams for you**. Brainstorm and write more ideas down, and before you know it, you'll have an acre of diamonds in your backyard. Enjoy!

Chapter 22 _____

Your Golden Signature

"Now yez listen to me, James Hawkins! You have the makins
of greatness in ye! But ye have to chart your course. Stick to
it. No matter the squall! And when the time comes to test
the true cut of your sails, well, I just hope I'm there catchin'
some of the light coming off ye!"

— Disney's *Treasure Planet*

When you look at Disney's empire, there's a tendency to
think, "This man had it easy! He got all the breaks!" But you'd
be wrong.

Unless you study the history of his entertainment regime,
you wouldn't know that Walt failed miserably dozens of times
before he founded Walt Disney Studios. Walt admitted that
he was much more comfortable in chaos than when things
were going right. But when things were downright crappy, his
brother Roy advised him to file for bankruptcy.

> *Walt Disney failed miserably before he founded Walt Disney Studios. When things were downright crappy, his brother advised him to file for bankruptcy. But he forged ahead.*

Walt forged ahead. Roy once said, "Tomorrow was always going to be the answer to all his problems." There's a lesson here.

Most people run from any sign of turbulence. Most people sulk when they are up against a wall. Most people throw in the towel way before they should.

My aim here is to lift you past that initial barrier in your mind when you say,

"This isn't fun anymore."
"This is impossible."
"I'm getting nowhere."
"This is not for me."

You can apply this story about Walt's plight to your fitness program, your business, and even to a struggling relationship. The key is to **keep your feet on the ground and your head in the clouds**.

As a young man, Walt practiced his signature countless times because he dreamed of seeing it as his brand and up in lights. Maybe that's why the Disney logo is so full of energy. Walt had practiced it a thousand times.

Here's another way to think about this little gem of a story. I turned my financial ship around not too long ago in pretty much the same way.

I write my goals in a power journal every night before going to bed. At one point, every few weeks, instead of goals, I'd write my signature over and over until the entire page was filled. **I visualized signing the back of many, many checks, big and small**. I visualized autographing books for fans. The energy and force coming off the page from this exercise filled me with excitement and enthusiasm to reach my goals.

> *This is the difference between people who reach the mountaintop of their dreams and those who get halfway up and then decide to turn around.*

You can do this exercise many ways and benefit from it. Maybe you want to buy your dream house. While writing your signature, visualize the closing process and signing all the documents. If you do this with great energy, it amplifies the effect that much more.

There are countless ways to take advantage of this technique. Just start by filling a page of paper with your signature, and then watch what happens to your confidence and your bank account.

This nugget is the difference between people who reach the mountaintop of their dreams and those who get halfway up and then decide to turn around because the air is a little thin and their feet hurt. When you keep dreams alive in your head, this practice lessens the pain and eases frustration a helluva lot.

Keep dreaming.

Fill the next page with your "golden signature"!

Chapter 23 _____/

Doodling Disney World

By the time he was 65, Walt Disney had become a well-known filmmaker, and his organization had taken animated films to a highly entertaining level. He began to finalize two more dreams: creating Disney World and EPCOT, the world of tomorrow.

Disney had no previous experience in real landscape development, but he wanted to learn all he could from the California Disneyland and incorporate it into this new park, since there was no precedent for what he wanted to create.

Walt Disney sketched the layout for his new Florida theme park on a napkin – while he was terminally ill. He could see it so clearly that a reporter once lay in bed next to him, jotting

down notes as Disney "mapped out" the entire plan on the
ceiling tiles above him.

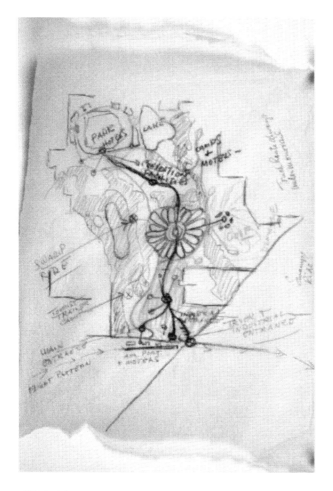

Walt Disney's original sketch for Disney World

This sketch looks like a bunch of scribbles and circles, mixing
in a few colors. It appears to be something that anyone could
create while talking on the phone and doodling away.

Yet, this exact plan became what we now know as Disney World. And it started with an idea that then became a sketch. Walt's vision for this new park could easily have been cast aside by the architects and land planners. But since there was a physical idea sketched out on paper for other people to work from, it blossomed into what Walt had envisioned in his mind in his last few years.

There is a powerful force that moves you closer to your vision if you just take time to put your thoughts onto paper.

Dream Doodling as Seen in the Movies

A while back, I watched the movie *Up* with my three girls. Pixar did it again, with another gem story and movie. We meet a couple who grows old together and has a dream of one day traveling the world. The wife paints a picture of their dream and hangs it over the fireplace. If you look closely, you see that she painted a house at the top of a waterfall in an exotic, mysterious place in South America. If you've seen the movie, you may have overlooked this golden moment in the story. You see, this is the couple's aspiration to get to Paradise Falls one day.

Granted, this is an animated film, but the story came from another person – not me. And it's fascinating to see this concept come alive in a movie. If you haven't seen it, (and I recommend it), watch for this scene, and think about what you've read in this chapter. The pictures are on the next page.

Screen captures taken from the movie Up! © Disney 2009

Chapter 24

How to Protect Your Family and Yourself

I met a friend the other day at a local coffee shop to "talk business." Before we got started on business, though, we had a heart-to-heart discussion on a topic that I want to share – because the origin of the topic is so magical.

Bill was my former art director, and he's a concept artist who can take anything in the world – complex or raw – and create an easy-to-understand picture about it. I got my first job in the U.S. with his help and we've stayed in contact over the years. One day we met for lunch, and we were talking about how to protect our kids on a day-to-day basis. Bill told me this story:

> When I was a kid, I lived on a farm. One hot, summer day when I was about 7, I was playing in a barn. I fell out of a two-story opening at the top and landed right on

my head. I got up, dusted myself off, and walked away. Now, I believe that I really should have died or at least been paralyzed by that fall. But because I was afraid that my mother would ban me from playing in the barn, I never told her about this.

My eyes grew wide as Bill shared the next piece of his mid-summer story. Years later, his brother, who knew about the fall, asked their mom if she'd heard that story. She had not, and she looked perplexed. And Bill waited for her to scold him, even at this ate date, for his behavior.

Instead, she said, "This is interesting. Every day when you two boys were little, **I would visualize a white bubble encasing you, and white light shining down on you**. I would do this once or twice a day. Your father never knew that I did this."

At that point, I realized that I'd heard all I needed to hear. Tears filled my eyes as I said something like, "Wow…simply amazing." Bill had truly had just divulged a heartfelt and miraculous story.

Not surprisingly, this inspired me, and I instantly thought of my girls and the times when I'm away from them. I'd been searching for something that I could do to keep them safe – and this type of visualization was the perfect solution.

There was a direct parallel here with coaching from my mentor, Matt Furey. Since I was so inspired and excited about this story, I decided to share this practice with you.

The Protection Exercise

1) Begin with three deep breaths. Hold the inhale for a count of 5, and then release it

2) Imagine a strong, powerful white light coming down from the heavens or through the universe.

3) See the light form a large bubble around your loved ones and yourself.

4) Visualize that image as you breathe deeply for four more cycles.

If you're concerned for your children's well-being, simply recall this visual instead of worrying. That way, you will be productive with your thought energy.

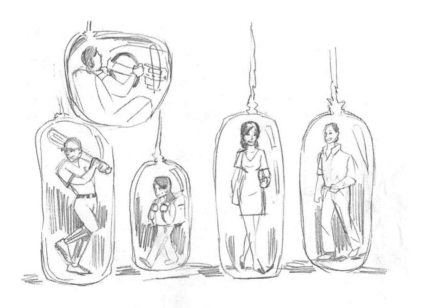

A Dream Doodle of how to visualize protectiing your family

Chapter 25 ————————/

Take Control of Your Thoughts to Cure Cancer in the Blink of an Eye

The names in this story have been changed to protect the individual's privacy.

A few months ago, I reconnected with an old high school and college friend on Facebook, and eventually we began talking on the phone. Susan is a teacher with a promising future ahead of her.

One day, I realized that I hadn't heard from her in quite a while. As it turned out, she was in the hospital with chicken pox. A few weeks later, she was back in the hospital, as doctors told her that she had a rare form of cancer in her breast and in her lung.

What do you say to someone who has been diagnosed with cancer, and of course, is feeling pretty depressed? Knowing what to say is even more difficult if you've never been in this type of situation.

Well, I retrieved a story that I'd heard by Norman Vincent Peale – a person who has had a major impact on my life. He told a story of positive mental imaging about a young woman who had been diagnosed with brain cancer. To combat this deadly disease, along with chemotherapy, **she visualized armies of white blood cells *lovingly* attacking the malignant brain tumor.** She visualized this over and over all day long. Like many other cancer recovery stories, she healed herself even though the future looked dismal and bleak.

So I decided to share this story with Susan, and she thanked me for the boost. But every time she went to see the doctor, she got more bad news. And second opinions were just as bad.

A few weeks later, I talked with her on the phone again. I could hear that the compounding bad news was taking its toll. Consequently, I told her examples of people who chose not to accept a doctor's thoughts on their state of affairs. Later in the conversation, she started feeling very sorry for herself and decided she would just drink herself into a drunken stupor.

Okay, not good. So I dug up one last story. I told her that if my aunt, a person who had smoked for 70 years, could overcome the deadly disease, then she could too. Since this young woman exercises and eats well, I told her that her condition was even more favorable. I could feel her heaviness lift a bit, and that was all I was trying to do.

A week or so passed and I texted her to ask how things were. She told me that her doctors said she had made an astounding recovery – that the lump in her breast was gone and the other nodes in her chest were not cancerous. She thanked me for the positive thinking, coaching, and healing energy that I'd sent her way.

Wow, imagine that! **And she *did* imagine that over and over**. She imagined being cancer-free. Her vision to be strong and healthy while attacking the cancerous tumor prevailed.

The interesting thing was that this combination of chemo and positive thought imaging blasted the cancer out of her life as quickly as it seemed to attack her.

"Keep the pressure on!" I told her before I hung up. "Keep thinking positively, and keep seeing your body ward off any unwanted intruders." Afterwards, I thought about what I could do to help her keep the errant potential negative thoughts from her doctors out of her head.

As a result, I resorted to my "bread and butter." I drew a castle that represented your mind – with you as the person guarding your mind of "stinking thinking." It includes a gatekeeper or guard from medieval days, I thought. This gatekeeper decides who and what is allowed into the castle. To help her see it clearly, I mailed this image to her.

Within just a couple of months, she was totally free of cancer. Turns out this combination attack of chemo, visualization, and positive thinking did the trick.

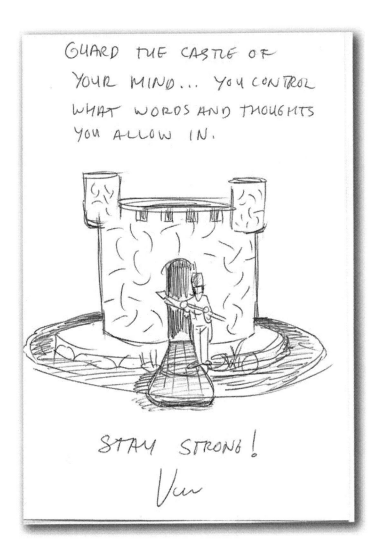

Chapter 26 ───────────/

A Magic Napkin Worth Money

Late in 1998, I returned home after my last year of playing football in Germany, and had spent a few weeks at my new corporate job. I was hired as a conceptual artist for a business learning company.

One day, I realized that my job wouldn't provide the income I expected. Maybe I thought I'd have a little more money left after taxes. And playing a pro sport had spoiled me a bit. In Germany, my house was paid for, my car was paid for... and practically everything I made went straight into my savings account.

But instead of whining about my situation, I planned my future and crafted it just as a sculptor does with clay. I made a clear, mental picture of what I wanted to create. I sketched the dream on paper. And then I took a step in the direction of my future.

Constructing Your Six-Figure Napkin

One day I went to lunch alone. In the back corner of Taco Bell, I made this lunchtime a fun, engaging, optimistic future planning session. (I've found that food makes me more creative, but that's just me.) You could do this anywhere, any time.

- I drew 5 lines across the middle of the napkin.
- Next to each space, I wrote the year, starting with 2000 – the year after the current one.
- On the first line, I wrote that year's income at $10,000 above what I was currently making.
- Then I skipped the next three lines and wrote $100,000 on the fifth line. I had always wanted to make this amount, and writing it on the napkin lifted my spirits.
- Then above the final line, I wrote in the number in for three of the middle lines and equally spaced out what seemed to be a logical amount of income per year.
- Finally, I sketched stick figures of myself crafting my future. As I ate, I thought of a metaphor to illustrate the progression from where I was to where I was going.

To summarize, I started with what was reasonable for my first year's goal. Then, **I stretched myself far more for the final year** in the last goal line. This is key to progressively push your mind past the current revenue thermometer in your mind.

What separates me from most self-improvement experts is the visual nature of the Law of Attraction process. **No one**

else teaches people to include stick figures and doodles along with your goals.

Plus, everyone can doodle. This one below proves you don't have to use complex realistic images, either.

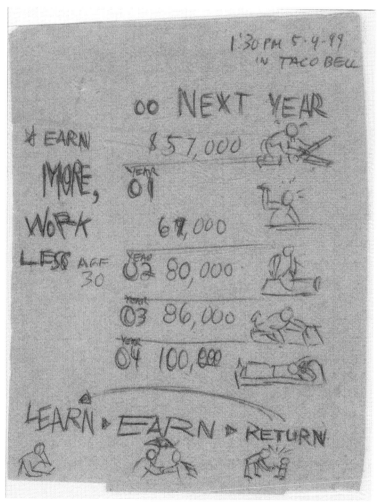

My financial Dream Doodle for yearly salary goals

The stick figures make the process fun. And more important, the image feeds your subconscious mind **instructions in a language it can understand**. Our minds think in terms of pictures. The cartoon guys showed me working and progressively constructing a beach chair so I could sit back and relax a bit.

And if you analyze the cartoon, next to the last year, you'll see that I believed I'd be living in the lap of luxury. I drew myself lying in a beach lounger just relaxing...ha! I thought I'd be well off and not have to think about money ever again.

Now, wouldn't you know...each and every year I made or exceeded the amount I scribbled on the napkin – ultimately leading up to that last year making over $100,000.

As I drew in the last panel, what seemed an impossible number to achieve was accomplished! And this is exciting! Any dream is possible if you map out a stair-step plan to reach a seemingly impossible figure.

> *Visuals of stick figures align every cell in your body to score your personal touchdown.*

Now if you're thinking you can't draw, think again. **The person who taught me to draw (my passionate Italian mother) said, "Everyone is an artist."** All you need is stick figures. This activates your subconscious mind. And just like a football coach drawing plays on the whiteboard so the entire team is on the same page, visuals of stick figures align every cell in your body to score your personal touchdown.

You're a Money Magnet

Some time ago, I invested in several courses on how to attract great wealth. These books and tapes were excellent tools for planting the seeds of prosperity in my mind.

Many themes were taught, but one in particular drove me to record it in the form of a visual – imagining myself as a "money magnet." It's a wonderful concept to toy around with. We all know how effortlessly a magnet attracts metal. When I drew this picture, I wanted to show how our minds are much like magnets, just by the nature of the thoughts we keep. And there is no better thought to hold in your mind than being a living, breathing magnet.

In this image, dollar bills are flying through the air and sticking to the figure in the middle. This man is holding up gold bars. There is a stack of gold behind him. Thousands of hundred-dollar bills are piling up at his feet.

If you want to try this, place this image next to your computer or some other place where you'll see it every second of the day. Read the title over and over. Cut out a picture of yourself and paste it on top of this figure so it's personalized for you.

Start to see and feel the money flowing to you easily and effortlessly. When you see it in your mind countless times, you won't be surprised when it falls out of the sky, seemingly "out of nowhere." That's because you will have seen this "happen" many times before.

Chapter 27 _____/

How I Manifested $3,450.35 in Four Hours

As you continue to practice working mindpower and Law of Attraction skills, you will undoubtedly improve. This means that things will arrive at your doorstep more quickly.

Here's a fun story about a little experiment I did one morning while working out.

I took my daughter to school and headed to a local hill to do some sprinting. The hill itself was about 50 to 60 yards, with a flatter surface that was about 20 yards long. I did 15 hill sprints with everything I had in the tank. Then I walked them three more times. Showing just what is in the illustration,

> *I carried an imaginary bubble in front of me holding my intention while I continued to walk the hill.*

I carried an imaginary bubble in front of me holding my intention while I continued to walk the hill. In this

The meditation process used for manifesting money fast

position, I said out loud, "I am now attracting $5,000 into my bank account from business services rendered."

Yes, my goal was to playfully see if I could generate $5,000 in one day. Sure, others have made far more in a day. But this isn't about them – it's about where I am in my own development. So I kept affirming this in different ways. Key point: *I said it out loud!*

I'd add things like, **"I'm so happy and grateful that I've attracted this into my life that I feel on top of the world!"**

By this time, I'd have reached the top of the hill. I'd look out and say it again, "I feel on top of the world! I had such an empowering feeling, and while gazing at the clear blue sky and green trees in the valley, I playfully experimented with this notion, and nothing seemed forced.

I finished my workout around 8 am. I wrote an email for my fitness community around 10. At exactly 11:03, I got an email (unrelated to the one I had just sent) with this in the subject line: **cartoon needed.**

The email read: "Can you please call me ASAP? Got an idea for a cartoon I would like to implement."

I called the customer, and it led to a sizable chunk of business. **Between that and another order that arrived on the same day, I made $3,450.63.**

Now, even though my initial email was unrelated to the response, the universe still rewarded a step in the direction of taking action! The email was a signal to the universe that I planned to do my part to make this manifestation happen.

And you say was this just a coincidence? I beg to differ, and I repeat, I don't believe in coincidences. **Everything happens for a reason.**

Give this little experiment a try. You just may be pleasantly surprised.

Chapter 28 ⎯⎯⎯⎯⎯⎯⎯

Creating Your Own Dream Doodles

Like the sketches I created to become a champion athlete, this same method can apply to the dreams you set for yourself. And as my sculpture teacher told me so many years ago, if you can imagine what you want to create and then draw it on paper, you can bring it to life in the form of a three-dimensional object.

I believe the same principle applies to the Law of Attraction. Like a sculpture creates something from nothing, I believe you too can create something out of thin air. You start from nothing, and in the end, you have a tangible object that is realized.

So we will begin with the end in mind. Start with what you want to achieve.

Do you want to lose weight?
Do you want more prosperity flowing into your life?
Do you want to balance your life better?

Do you want to bond more with your child?
Do you want to attract someone into your life?

Whatever the goal, choose one thing to focus on, and then create a stick-figure picture that illustrates the theme you want to bring into your life.

Whatever you can doodle, you can do. When you put yourself in creator mode, you go from helpless victim to a person in control. This approach helps you take a proactive role in creating the life you want, rather than reacting, where life happens to you. Now go tackle your dreams!

Creating Your Six-Figure Stick Figure

Start a new habit: doodle your dreams daily. You'll mold and shape your mind for success in the future. And you can do this while you're on the phone, waiting in the doctor's office or hair salon, or watching TV.

Select anything you want to achieve. I will provide instructions for creating a simple image and then add your financial goal. This will amplify your written goals, if you have them, or stir excitement for a new process if you don't.

I've heard many times through the years people say, "Wow, you are an artist? I can't even draw a stick figure."

No? Well, turn the page and let's dive right in. I'll show you how.

1. Draw a circle for the head.

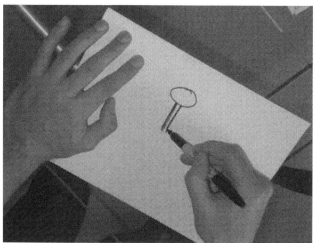

2. Draw a line for the body.
Add a second line to give it more form, if you like.

3. Add legs and feet.

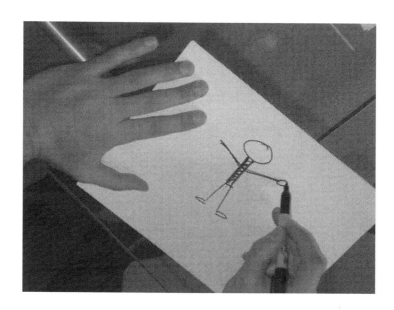

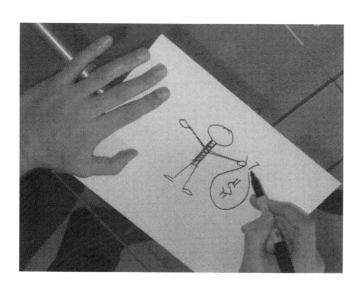

5. Add arms, hands, and bags of money!

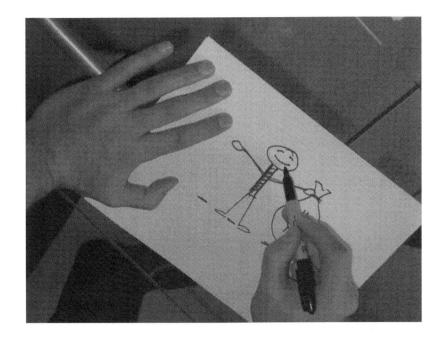

**6. Write your goal under your moneybag.
And then finish it off with a smile!**

You'll end up with this.
(You can even trace this one. I won't tell anybody.)

Now, repeat this every day until you hit that goal!
Sometimes you have to remind your mind what you
want *over and over* before it *get's* the picture.

SPECIAL DREAM DOODLE COACHING OFFER!

What Is Your Dream, Buried Deep, that Begs to be Unleashed?

Vince can help you attract
more money,
a soulmate,
health and vitality,
a new career,
your dream home,
and much more!

If you would like to work one-on-one with Vince Palko to create your personalized Dream Doodle, send an email to vince@vincepalko.com

Vince is flexible, easy to work with, and loves helping people to blast past their perceived personal limits.

Visit VincePalko.com to sign up for his *free* Health and Wealth newsletter!

Acknowledgements

My mother and father have much to do with my success. Both showered me with praise, support, and love every step of the way. You have blessed me 1,000 times over.

I'm grateful for my mentors and coaches through the years: Jim Anderson, Matt Furey, Gary Blackney, Paul Ferraro, Steve Telander, Gary Palmer, Jeff Palmer, Jim Merlitti, John Cistone, Dan Boarman, Daegan Smith, and David Smith. I'm grateful to my excellent teachers of art and design: Sean Morin, Carol Leibowitz, Mark Zust, Bill Hinsch, Victor Zhang, and Cory Barba.

Thanks go to Best SellingCovers.com for its cover design and layout. I'd also like to thank my editor, Veronica Hughes, for her amazing support in launching this book off the runway (WriteThereWithYou.com).

I would be remiss if I didn't thank my three lovely girls. You continue to teach me, and I love you to the moon and back a trillion times. I could not have done this without any of you. Many, many thanks!

About the author

Vince Palko is a lover of motivational and inspiring books, audio, and video. His goal is to share the ranks of Norman Vincent Peale, Brian Tracy, Bob Proctor, Joe Vitale, Tony Robbins, and other prolific authors and speakers to mold the self-development landscape with his unique stamp. This is Vince's third self-

development book, along with *Tackling Life's Problems* and *Gridiron Mind Power*. Vince is the father of three wonderfully adorable little girls, Sophia, Georgia, and Vivian, all under the age of 10. When Dad grows up, he wants to be just like them!

About the illustrator

One of Vince Palko's first loves was picking up a pen to create artwork. He has never stopped allowing his inner child to roam freely. Drawing allowed this strong connection with his inner child to grow younger every day. Vince feels blessed to have the ability to visually express what he sees in his mind's eye easily and effortlessly. His goal is to help millions of others do the same until they reach their dreams.

Made in the USA
Columbia, SC
11 September 2021